GOING BUGGY!

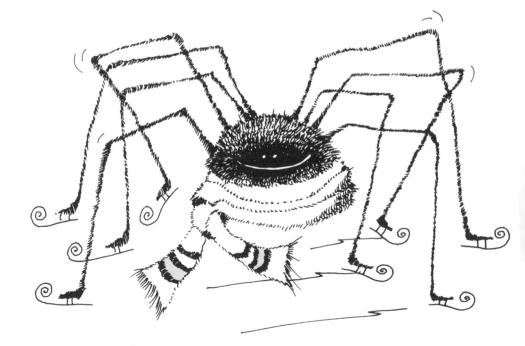

Make Me Laugh!

GOING BUGGY!

jokes about insects

by Peter & Connie Roop / pictures by Joan Hanson

Lerner Publications Company · Minneapolis

For Heidi, our lovely "lady-bug"

Library of Congress Cataloging-in-Publication Data

Roop, Peter.
  Going buggy!

  (Make me laugh!)
  Summary: A collection of jokes and riddles about
insects, including "What do you call a bug dance? A
moth ball."
  1. Insects—Juvenile humor. 2. Wit and humor,
Juvenile. 3. Riddles, Juvenile. [1. Insects—Wit
and humor. 2. Jokes. 3. Riddles] I. Roop, Connie.
II. Hanson, Joan, ill. III. Title. IV. Series.
PN6231.I56R66   1986   818'.5402   86-2941
ISBN 0-8225-0988-1 (lib. bdg.)

Manufactured in the United States of America

1 2 3 4 5 6 7 8 9 10 96 95 94 93 92 91 90 89 88 87 86

Q: What do young insects ride in?
A: Baby buggies.

Q: What kind of insects can dance?
A: Jitter-bugs.

Q: What do you call a bug dance?
A: A moth ball.

Q: What does a tick attack?
A: A tick attacks a toe.

Q: What kind of bug has no wings but flies?
A: A spider.

Q: Why did the spider spin a web?
A: She didn't know how to knit one.

Q: Which bug is related to you?
A: Your ant.

Q: What did the mother grasshopper say
to her children?
A: "Hop to it!"

Q: What kind of insect sleeps the most?
A: A bedbug.

Q: How does a bee brush its hair?
A: With its honeycomb.

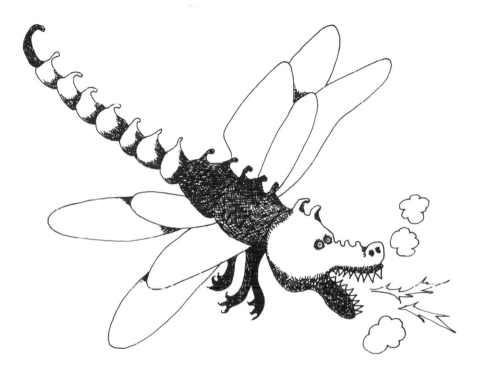

Q: What kind of bugs do knights fight?
A: Dragonflies.

Q: What kind of bugs can you find in a clock?
A: Ticks.

Q: What language do ticks speak?
A: Tick talk.

Q: What do you call a tired centipede?
A: A sleepy creepy.

Q: What did the boy say to the mosquito?
A: "Don't bug me!"

Diner: What is this spider doing in my soup?
Waiter: The backstroke!

Q: What kind of bugs are the sweetest?
A: Honeybees.

Q: What kind of insects are the best singers?
A: Hum-bugs.

Q: What is the name of a famous bug rock group?
A: The Beetles.

Q: What kind of music do the Beetles play?
A: Bee-bop.

Q: How are bugs and babies alike?
A: They both creep and crawl.

Q: Which sport do mosquitoes like the best?
A: Skin diving.

Q: What has 18 legs and catches flies?
A: A baseball team.

Q: What do you call the head of a roach
basketball team?
A: The roach coach.

Q: Why do bugs hate baseball bats?
A: Because they're fly swatters.

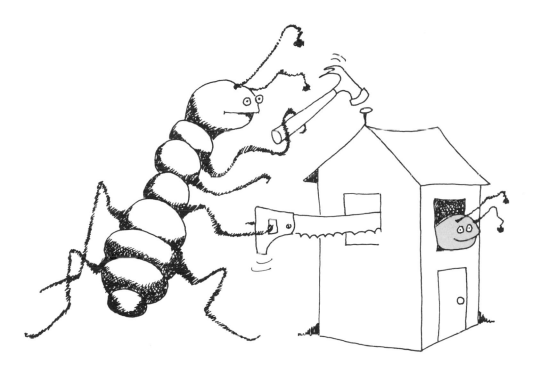

Q: What kind of insects are the best builders?
A: Carpenter ants.

Q: What kind of bugs do you find in church?
A: Praying mantises.

Q: What kind of insects are always polite?
A: Ladybugs.

Q: What did the boy centipede say to the girl centipede?
A: "I want to hold your hand, hand, hand, hand, hand, ..."

Q: What do you call a young bee?
A: A babe-bee.

Q: Why did the boy throw the butter out of the window?

A: He wanted to see a butter-fly.

Q: What has four wheels and flies?

A: A garbage truck.

Mary: What has 18 feet, red eyes, and long claws?

Sue: I don't know, what?

Mary: I don't know either, but it's crawling up your neck!

Q: What happened when the bald man saw a centipede?

A: It was a hair-raising experience.

Q: Where can you buy bugs?
A: At a flea market.

Q: Why can't you weigh a firefly?
A: Because it's so light.

Q: What kind of insect uses a camera?
A: A shutter-bug.

Q: What worm can never go into space?
A: An earthworm.

Q: What kind of ants are the biggest?
A: Gi-ants.

Q: When did the fly fly?
A: When the spider spied-her.

Q: Which insect has a hard time making up its mind?
A: A may-bee.

Q: Why are bees so rich?
A: They "cell" their honey.

Q: What kind of insects are the smartest?
A: Fireflies—because they're so bright.

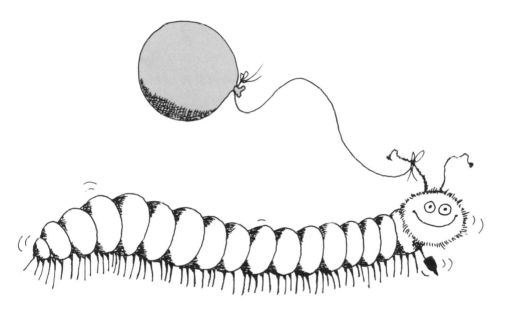

Q: What goes 99-thump, 99-thump, 99-thump?
A: A centipede with a wooden leg.

Q: What kind of bug does a cowboy ride?
A: A horsefly.

Q: How do you start a firefly race?
A: Ready, set, GLOW!

Q: What kind of insects do campers like best?
A: Fireflies.

Q: How do you hunt for bees?
A: With a bee-bee gun.

Q: What does a cotton farmer call a bad beetle?
A: An evil weevil.

Q: What is worse than finding a worm in your apple?

A: Finding half a worm in your apple.

Q: Which bug can you find in the alphabet?

A: B.

Q: What kind of insects are good in school?

A: Spelling bees.

Q: What kind of bugs are the messiest?

A: Litter-bugs.

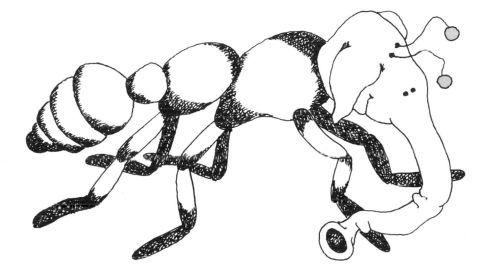

Q: What kind of ants have trunks?
A: Eleph-ants.

Q: What kind of insects are dirty?
A: Grubs.

Q: Who is the king of the insects?
A: The monarch.

Nate knew a gnu that had gnats,
Which gnawed him whenever he sat.
To get rid of these pests,
He wore bug-proof vests,
Which is good news for gnus who have gnats.

Q: What does a moth sleep on?
A: A cater-pillow.

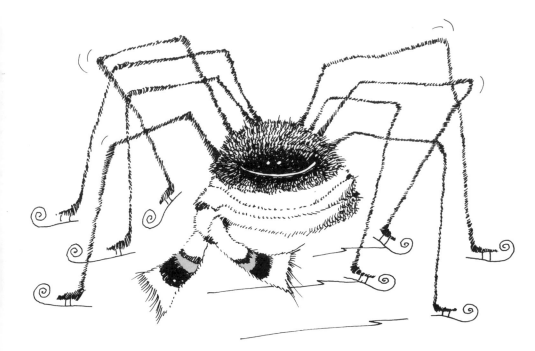

ABOUT THE AUTHORS

PETER AND CONNIE ROOP have enjoyed sharing jokes with students in the United States and Great Britain. When not joking around, Peter and Connie write books and articles. Traveling, camping, and reading with their children, Sterling and Heidi, are their favorite pastimes. Both graduates of Lawrence University, the Roops now live in Appleton, Wisconsin.

ABOUT THE ARTIST

JOAN HANSON lives with her husband and two sons in Afton, Minnesota. Her distinctive, deliberately whimsical pen-and-ink drawings have illustrated more than 30 children's books. Ms. Hanson is also an accomplished weaver. A graduate of Carleton College, Hanson enjoys tennis, skiing, sailing, reading, traveling, and walking in the woods surrounding her home.

Make Me Laugh!

101 ANIMAL JOKES
101 FAMILY JOKES
101 KNOCK-KNOCK JOKES
101 MONSTER JOKES
101 SCHOOL JOKES
101 SPORTS JOKES
CAT'S OUT OF THE BAG!
GO HOG WILD!

GOING BUGGY!
GRIN AND BEAR IT!
IN THE DOGHOUSE!
LET'S CELEBRATE!
OUT TO LUNCH!
SPACE OUT!
STICK OUT YOUR TONGUE!